You Can Recycle!

by Patricia Walsh

PEARSON
Scott
Foresman

DK

What You Already Know

Everything we need and use comes from Earth. Each of these things is called a natural resource. Some natural resources, called renewable resources, can be replaced during our lifetimes. For instance, trees are a renewable resource. While you are alive, a young tree will grow into an adult tree, replacing another tree that has been used.

Some of our natural resources, called nonrenewable resources, cannot be replaced during our lifetimes. Oil and coal, which are found beneath the Earth's surface, are nonrenewable resources. The oil we use cannot be replaced during our lifetimes.

A few resources are never used up. They are sunlight, wind, and water.

wind farm

items ready for recycling

We need to be careful not to waste or use up our natural resources. We also need to be careful not to damage or spoil our air and water. Using our natural resources wisely is called conservation. When we reuse and recycle our natural resources, we are also helping to conserve another natural resource, our land. When we find a way to keep our trash from filling up landfills, we are helping to conserve land.

Natural resources are important to all living things. How we use and reuse our natural resources affects our life on Earth. Read on to find out how to recycle in a way that will help our planet!

Facts About Trash

The average American creates about four pounds of trash each day. Our country produces 210 million tons of trash each year. Where does it go?

More than half of our trash is buried in landfills. A landfill is a large area where trash is discarded. This trash spreads out and piles high, taking up a lot of space. It is expensive for cities to haul trash to landfills. Landfills also fill up quickly because the trash in them does not decompose well.

Landfills take up a large amount of space and are costly to run.

Here's the good news: Americans are recycling and composting more than 25 percent of their trash! Metal, glass, and plastic can all be recycled. When we recycle them, they get changed into things we can use again.

Everything here can be recycled.

Composting is similar to recycling. Natural yard and kitchen waste gets composted, meaning it gets returned to the soil.

On the following pages you'll read about materials that can be recycled. You'll also learn about the energy saved by recycling and how recycling makes the environment cleaner!

It's important to learn which recyclable items go in which recycling bins.

Aluminum

These aluminum cans are being sent into a recycling plant.

About 100 billion aluminum cans are made in the United States each year. Of that number, about half are recycled. For every aluminum can that gets recycled, one less can has to be made from new materials.

Natural resources are conserved when aluminum is recycled. It takes four pounds of bauxite ore to make one pound of aluminum. Less ore needs to be mined from the Earth when more aluminum is recycled.

When you drop an aluminum can into a recycling bin, you have helped recycle aluminum! Scrap metal companies collect the cans and crush them into large bales. The bales are then shredded into small pieces and melted.

How Aluminum Can Be Recycled

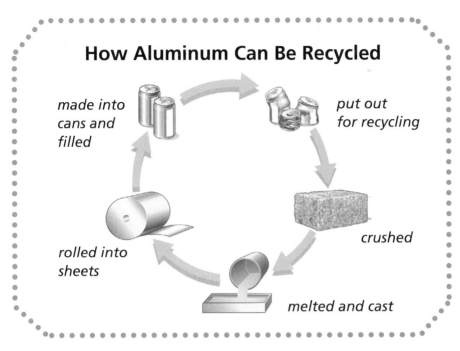

made into cans and filled

put out for recycling

crushed

melted and cast

rolled into sheets

After that, the recycled aluminum is blended with new aluminum and poured into huge bars. Rolling mills press the bars into thin sheets. Finally, the sheets are formed into new cans.

By recycling aluminum cans, you stop them from becoming trash and taking up space in a landfill.

New aluminum cans are made from poured, melted metal.

Paper

The average U.S. resident uses 749 pounds of paper each year. Books, magazines, newspapers, and many other things are made of paper. Thanks to recycling programs, Americans now recycle more paper than they throw away.

When you separate paper from other trash, you have helped recycle paper! That paper is then sent to recycling centers. The centers sort it and remove plastic and paper clips.

Tons and tons of paper get recycled each year in the United States.

After the paper has been sorted, it is formed into thousand-pound bundles and sent to mills. At the mills, the recycled paper is soaked in water and chemicals. This causes the paper to separate into fibers, or pulp. The pulp is then filtered through screens.

This worker is inspecting a new roll of recycled paper.

At the same time, the ink from newspapers and magazines is removed. The clean, recycled pulp is then mixed with new wood pulp to make new paper products.

Unlike aluminum, paper cannot be recycled again and again. After repeated recycling, paper fibers get so small that they slip through the screens. At that point, the fibers become waste and have to be composted, burned, or taken to a landfill.

These newspapers have been recycled so many times they are waste.

Plastic

Many things you use are made of plastic. Fortunately, much of that plastic can be recycled!

When you drop things made of plastic into the recycling bin, you have helped recycle plastic! Collectors then wash and chop the plastic into flakes. The flakes are then dried and melted. Then the melted plastic is forced through a screen to remove toxins and form new plastic strands. The strands are cooled and chopped into pellets. Plastic pellets are used to make items such as flowerpots and carpets.

It's important to learn the basics of plastic recycling.

Glass

Many people throw away glass bottles and jars. It's too bad, because glass can be recycled to make new glass!

When you place glass into bins, you have helped recycle it! Collectors go around picking up that glass. The glass is separated by color. The color in brown and green glass cannot be removed. So recycled glass that is colored can only make more colored glass.

The glass is broken into small pieces called cullet. After that, the cullet is crushed, sorted, cleaned, and mixed with other raw materials to make new glass. Recycled glass can be made into new jars and bottles. Best of all, glass can be recycled again and again!

Glass recycling bins like these teach people to sort glass materials.

Organic Waste

Many people have turned to composting as a way to recycle organic yard waste. Organic yard waste includes grass clippings and leaves that might otherwise be thrown into a landfill. Organic kitchen waste can be composted too. This includes coffee grounds,

Organic materials include fruits and vegetables.

eggshells, potato peels, and apple cores. Compost made of organic yard waste and kitchen waste will produce a rich soil that can be used in any garden!

Worms help the composting of food and yard wastes. The worms process the food waste and yard waste through their bodies. The compost that comes out makes great soil.

These three photos show how a red pepper naturally turns into compost after only fifteen days.

day 1　　　　day 8　　　　day 15

How Organic Waste Can Be Recycled

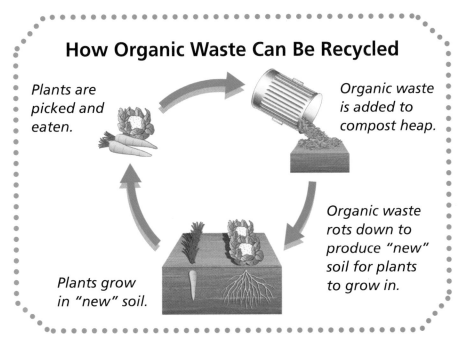

Plants are picked and eaten.

Organic waste is added to compost heap.

Organic waste rots down to produce "new" soil for plants to grow in.

Plants grow in "new" soil.

It is expensive for cities and towns to throw away the organic waste that we produce. Even though organic waste is made entirely of natural materials, it can take years to decompose in landfills. When we recycle organic waste into compost, we return the organic matter to the soil. This means less trash filling up our landfills!

A good compost heap will produce thick, rich garden soil.

Recycling The Right Way

Right now you might be asking, "What can I do to reduce trash in the landfills and protect our environment?" Just put the three Rs of Reduce, Reuse, and Recycle into your daily life! Fortunately, it is very easy to do.

Reduce means using only what you really need. Don't be wasteful. Reuse means using something as much as possible before throwing it away. Always ask yourself, "Can I reuse this?"

Recycling Symbols

These symbols are used worldwide to indicate that a material can be recycled.

It's important to separate different types of recycling materials.

Recycle means finding out about your community's recycling program and recycling your aluminum, paper, plastic, and glass trash. Find out where your nearest recycling center is. Collect recyclables and take them to the recycling center. Recycle yard waste and kitchen waste by composting. In order to help with community composting, some communities collect yard waste separately from the regular trash collection. Check to see if your community does this.

When we recycle, we help take care of the Earth, right in our homes. So make sure to recycle as much as you can. It's fun and easy to do!

It's easy to start recycling.

Glossary

compost   decomposing organic waste used for fertilizing the soil

cullet   pieces of crushed glass that are added to other materials in order to make new glass

discarded   tossed aside after it is no longer useful

landfill   structure built into or on top of the ground where trash is stored

ore   minerals from which metal can be taken out, usually for profit

pulp   ground-up, moistened fibers of wood or recycled paper used to make new paper

toxin   a substance that is harmful to living things